Kim Schaefer

BLACK & WHITE
BRIGHT & BOLD

24 Quilt Projects to Piece & Appliqué

C&T PUBLISHING

Text copyright © 2013 by Kim Schaefer

Photography and Artwork copyright © 2013 by C&T Publishing, Inc.

Publisher: Amy Marson

Creative Director: Gailen Runge

Art Director: Kristy Zacharias

Editor: Lynn Koolish

Technical Editors: Helen Frost and Susan Hendrickson

Cover Designer: Kristen Yenche

Book Designer: April Mostek

Production Coordinators: Zinnia Heinzmann and Jenny Davis

Production Editors: Alice Mace Nakanishi and Katie Van Amburg

Illustrator: Wendy Mathson

Photo Assistant: Mary Peyton Peppo

Photography by Diane Pedersen and Nissa Brehmer of C&T Publishing, Inc., unless otherwise noted

Published by C&T Publishing, Inc., P.O. Box 1456, Lafayette, CA 94549

Library of Congress Cataloging-in-Publication Data

Schaefer, Kim, 1960-

 Black & white, bright & bold : 24 quilt projects to piece & appliqué / Kim Schaefer.

   pages cm

 ISBN 978-1-60705-786-4 (soft cover)

1. Quilting--Patterns. 2. Patchwork. 3. Appliqué. I. Title. II. Title: Black and white, bright and bold.

 TT835.S2825 2013

 746.46--dc23

                     2013009778

Printed in China

10 9 8 7 6 5 4 3 2 1

Acknowledgments

For many years now, I have had the pleasure of working with the talented team of people at C&T Publishing. My genuine thanks go to all of you for your continued support and dedication to publishing the best books possible.

Special thanks to:

Lynn Koolish—my editor; once again it has been my pleasure to work with you.

Helen Frost—my technical editor; thank you so much for your diligence in checking and rechecking all my work for accuracy. Technical editing is such a difficult job and you are so talented at it. I am extremely grateful for everything you do.

Wendy Mathson—for the beautiful illustrations.

Diane Minkley of Patched Works, Inc.—my truly awesome longarm quilter. Thank you again for finishing my quilts so beautifully.

Julie Karasek and the Patched Works ladies—Julie, thank you for your continued support. Jen, Lisa, and the entire staff, thank you for your smiles and hellos when I walk in the door, even though you know I will make a mess and have you cutting ¼-yard cuts off many, many bolts of fabric.

Gary Schaefer—my husband; thank you for all you do for me. You're the best.

CONTENTS

INTRODUCTION

I have always enjoyed quilts made from black-and-white fabrics. I also like black-and-white fabrics in combination with one other color or several other colors. The high contrast between the fabrics allows for visually stunning quilts. As with quilts made from solid fabrics, black-and-white quilts have a boldness and beauty that is timeless. Often quilts made with black-and-white fabrics have a contemporary feeling regardless of when they were made.

In the book I have used not only "true" black-and-white fabrics but also black and off-white or cream, as in *Licorice Medley Lap Quilt* (page 12) and *Tile Works Lap Quilt* (page 20). *Berry Vine Runner* (page 48) also uses these fabrics. Generally, true black-and-white fabrics create quilts with a bolder, more graphic, more modern look, while the black-and-cream (or off-white) fabrics create quilts with a softer, more subdued feeling.

This book contains a collection of 24 different projects, including lap quilts, wall quilts, runners, and place mats in both pieced and appliquéd designs for you to choose from.

I have thoroughly enjoyed designing this collection of projects. I hope this book will be a continued source of creativity and inspiration for you and that you will make some beautiful new quilts for your family and friends to enjoy.

—*Kim Schaefer*

GENERAL INSTRUCTIONS

Rotary Cutting Tools

I recommend that you cut all the fabrics used in the pieced blocks, borders, and bindings with a rotary cutter, acrylic ruler, and cutting mat. Trim the blocks and borders with these tools as well.

Piecing

All piecing measurements include ¼" seam allowances. If you sew an accurate ¼" seam you will succeed. My biggest and best quiltmaking tip is to learn to sew an accurate ¼" seam.

Pressing

Press seams to one side, preferably toward the darker fabric. Press flat and avoid sliding the iron over the pieces, which can distort and stretch them. When you join two seamed sections, press the seams in opposite directions so you can nest the seams and reduce bulk.

Appliqué

All appliqué instructions are for paper-backed fusible web with machine appliqué, and all the patterns have been drawn in reverse. If you prefer a different appliqué method, you will need to trace a mirror image of the pattern and add seam allowances to the appliqué pieces. A lightweight paper-backed fusible web works best for machine appliqué. Choose your favorite fusible web and follow the manufacturer's directions.

General Appliqué Instructions

1. Trace all the parts of the appliqué design on the paper side of the fusible web. Trace each layer of the design separately. Whenever 2 shapes in the design butt together, overlap them by about ⅛" to help prevent a gap from forming between them. When tracing the shapes, extend the underlapped edge ⅛" beyond the drawn edge in the pattern. Write the pattern letter or number on each traced shape.

2. Cut around the appliqué shapes, leaving a ¼" margin around each piece.

3. Iron each fusible web shape to the wrong side of the appropriate fabric, following the manufacturer's directions for fusing. I don't worry about the grainline when placing the pieces.

4. Cut on the traced lines and peel off the paper backing. A thin layer of fusible web will remain on the wrong side of the fabric. This layer will adhere the appliqué pieces to the backgrounds.

5. Position the pieces on the backgrounds. Press to fuse them in place.

6. Machine stitch around the appliqué pieces using a zigzag, satin, or blanket stitch. Stitch any detail lines indicated on the patterns. My choice is the satin stitch. I generally use matching threads for all the stitching. As always, the type of stitching you use and the thread color you select are personal choices.

Putting It All Together

When all the blocks are completed, arrange them on the floor or, if you are lucky enough to have one, a design wall. Arrange and rearrange the blocks until you are happy with the overall look. Each project has specific directions for assembly, as well as diagrams and photos.

Borders

If the quilt borders or lattice pieces need to be longer than 40", join crosswise strips of fabric at a 45° angle as necessary and cut the strips to the desired length. All the borders in the book are straight cut in the corners; none of them have mitered corners.

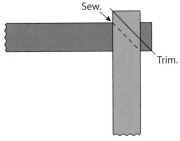

Sew. Trim. Join borders with 45° angle.

Layering the Quilt

Cut the batting and backing pieces 4"–5" larger than the quilt top on all sides. Place the pressed backing on the bottom, right side down. Place the batting over the backing and place the quilt top on top, right side up. Make sure all the layers are flat and smooth and the quilt top is centered over the batting and backing. Pin or baste the quilt.

Note: If you are going to have your top quilted by a longarm quilter, contact him or her for specific batting and backing requirements, as they may differ from the instructions above.

Quilting

Quilting is a personal choice; you may prefer hand or machine quilting. My favorite method is to send the quilt top to a longarm quilter. This method keeps my number of unfinished tops low and the number of finished quilts high.

Color and Fabric Choices

I have used 100% cotton fabrics in all the projects in this book. I find they are easy to work with, and they are readily available at your local quilt shop.

When using black-and-white fabrics in quilts, it is often important to have high contrast between or within the blocks for a pattern to be a success. In projects where I felt the contrast was essential to the overall look of the quilt, I differentiated between the black-and-white prints by listing them separately in the materials section. For example, when a black-and-white print has a predominantly light background it will be listed as "white-and-black print (light background)," and when a black-and-white print has a predominantly dark background it will be listed as "black-and-white print (dark background)." When there is no separate listing, feel free to use either black-and-white prints or white-and-black prints. You can also mix and match, as in *Peacock Feathers Lap Quilt* (page 15).

Several of the patterns use black and white in combination with another color. This color can always be successfully replaced with a color of your choice. I encourage you to embrace your own personal style and preferences. Color and fabric choices can dramatically affect a quilt's overall look. Through these choices you will be able to create something that reflects who you are.

Making the Quilt Your Own

If you want to change the size of a quilt, simply add or subtract blocks. To change the size of vertically oriented projects, such as *Making Tracks Lap Quilt* (page 8) or *Totally Stacked Lap Quilt* (page 23), the number of columns or the width of the lattice pieces can be altered. Many of the quilts are borderless, giving them a more contemporary look. If your preference is a more traditional look, adding borders can achieve this.

Yardage and Fabric Requirements

I have given yardage and fabric requirements for each project, with many calling for a total amount of assorted fabrics that can be used as a base for the quilt. The yardage amounts may vary depending on several factors: the size of the quilt, the number of fabrics used, and the number of pieces you cut from each fabric. When cutting strips for rectangles, I cut the narrower measurement first, then subcut the strip into the pieces needed. Always cut the pieces for the patchwork first; then cut any appliqué pieces.

The amounts given for binding allow for 2"-wide strips cut on the straight of grain. I usually use the same fabric for the backing and binding; it's a good way to use leftover fabric. Cut the binding strips on either the crosswise or lengthwise grain of the leftover fabric—whichever will yield the longest strips.

PROJECTS

MAKING TRACKS LAP QUILT

FINISHED BLOCKS: **A:** 9″ × 7″ **B:** 9″ × 5″ **C:** 9″ × 9″ **D:** 9″ × 2″ **E:** 9″ × 3″
FINISHED LAP QUILT: 63½″ × 83½″

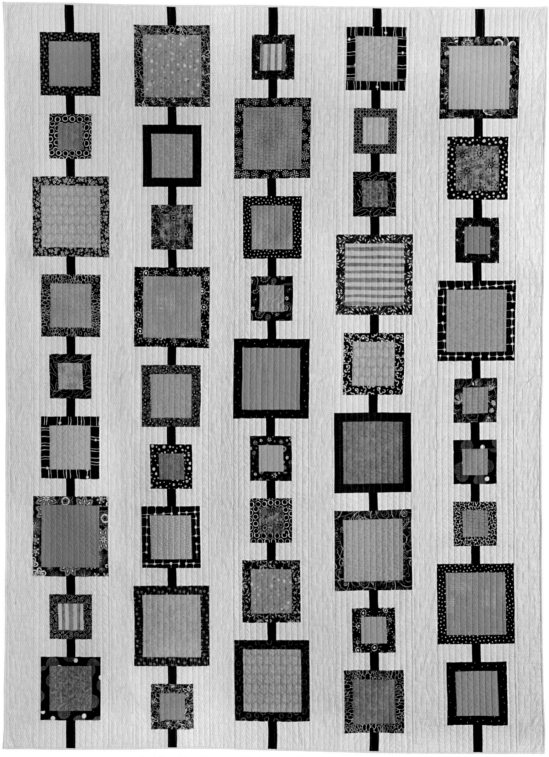

Quilted by Diane Minkley of Patched Works, Inc.

Black-and-white prints are used to frame the squares in this lap quilt. The light background gives this quilt a fresh, modern look. I chose assorted greens for the center squares, but I think several solids or larger-scale prints would work for this pattern as well.

MATERIALS

- 1½ yards total assorted greens for pieced blocks
- 1¾ yards total assorted black-and-white prints (dark backgrounds) for pieced blocks
- ¼ yard black for pieced blocks
- 3 yards light for pieced blocks and vertical lattice pieces
- 5½ yards for backing and binding
- 68″ × 88″ batting

CUTTING

Cut from assorted greens:
- 14 squares 5½″ × 5½″ for Block A
- 17 squares 3½″ × 3½″ for Block B
- 14 squares 7½″ × 7½″ for Block C

Cut from assorted black-and-white prints:
- 28 rectangles 1½″ × 5½″ for Block A
- 28 rectangles 1½″ × 7½″ for Block A
- 34 rectangles 1½″ × 3½″ for Block B
- 34 rectangles 1½″ × 5½″ for Block B
- 28 rectangles 1½″ × 7½″ for Block C
- 28 rectangles 1½″ × 9½″ for Block C

Cut from black:
- 44 rectangles 1½″ × 2½″ for Block D
- 6 rectangles 1½″ × 3½″ for Block E

Cut from light:
- 28 rectangles 1½″ × 7½″ for Block A
- 34 rectangles 2½″ × 5½″ for Block B
- 88 rectangles 2½″ × 4½″ for Block D
- 12 rectangles 3½″ × 4½″ for Block E
- 6 strips 3½″ × 83½″ (on lengthwise grain) for vertical lattice

PIECING

BLOCK A

Piece Block A as shown. Press. Make 14 blocks.

Block A: Step 1

Step 2

Step 3—Make 14 blocks.

BLOCK B

Piece Block B as shown. Press. Make 17 blocks.

Block B: Step 1

Step 2

Step 3—Make 17 blocks.

BLOCK C

Piece Block C as shown. Press. Make 14 blocks.

Block C: Step 1

Step 2—Make 14 blocks.

BLOCK D

Piece Block D as shown. Press. Make 44 blocks.

Block D—Make 44 blocks.

BLOCK E

Piece Block E as shown. Press. Make 6 blocks.

Block E—Make 6 blocks.

PUTTING IT ALL TOGETHER

1. Arrange and sew together the blocks into 5 vertical rows. Press.

2. Sew the vertical lattice pieces between the rows and on the sides to form the quilt top. Press.

FINISHING

1. Layer the quilt top with the batting and backing. Baste or pin.

2. Quilt as desired and bind.

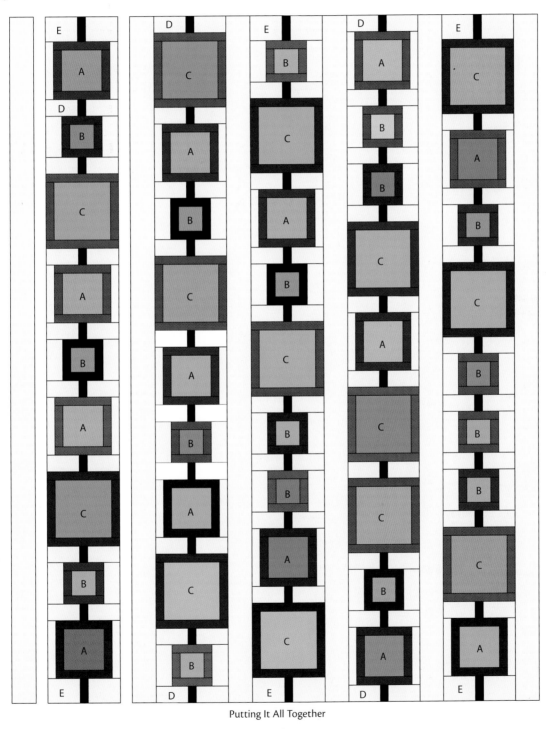

Putting It All Together

LICORICE MEDLEY LAP QUILT

FINISHED BLOCK: $8'' \times 8''$ • **FINISHED LAP QUILT:** $58\frac{1}{2}'' \times 74\frac{1}{2}''$

Quilted by Diane Minkley of Patched Works, Inc.

Black & White, Bright & Bold

The black-and-white prints in this quilt are actually black and cream, giving the quilt a softer, more subtle look. The pastels used for the pieced centers enhance the softer feeling of the quilt. This quilt reminds me of the licorice candy I ate as a child. For a more graphic look, use true black-and-white prints with bright center squares.

MATERIALS

- 1 yard total assorted pastels for pieced blocks
- 2¾ yards total assorted black-and-white prints for pieced blocks
- 1¾ yards black for pieced blocks and borders
- 4½ yards for backing and binding
- 63" × 79" batting

CUTTING

Cut from assorted pastels:
- 189 squares 2½" × 2½"

Cut from assorted black-and-white prints:
- 126 rectangles 1½" × 6½"
- 126 rectangles 2½" × 6½"

Cut from black:
- 126 rectangles 1½" × 8½" for pieced blocks
- 2 strips 1½" × 72½" for side borders
- 2 strips 1½" × 58½" for top and bottom borders

PIECING

Piece the blocks. Press. Make 63 blocks.

Step 1

Step 2

Step 3

Step 4—Make 63 blocks.

PUTTING IT ALL TOGETHER

QUILT CENTER

1. Arrange and sew together the blocks into 9 rows of 7 blocks each. Press.

2. Sew together the rows to form the quilt top. Press.

BORDER

1. Sew the 2 side borders to the quilt top. Press toward the borders.

2. Sew the top and bottom borders to the quilt top. Press toward the borders.

FINISHING

1. Layer the quilt top with the batting and backing. Baste or pin.

2. Quilt as desired and bind.

Putting It All Together

PEACOCK FEATHERS LAP QUILT

FINISHED BLOCK: 5″ × 4″ • **FINISHED LAP QUILT:** 60½″ × 84½″

Quilted by Diane Minkley of Patched Works, Inc.

MATERIALS

- 5 yards total assorted black-and-white prints for appliqué and pieced backgrounds
- 3½ yards total assorted greens and teals for appliquéd feathers
- 5¼ yards for backing and binding
- 8½ yards paper-backed fusible web
- 65″ × 89″ batting

CUTTING

Cut from assorted black-and-white prints:

- 168 rectangles 4½″ × 5½″ for appliqué backgrounds
- 168 rectangles 2½″ × 5½″ for pieced backgrounds

Teal and green fabrics are paired with black-and-white prints to create this appliquéd lap quilt.

APPLIQUÉING

Refer to Appliqué (page 5) as needed. Appliqué patterns are on pullout page P2.

1. Cut 84 of appliqué pieces 1 and 2. Cut 84 of appliqué pieces 1 and 2 reversed (1R and 2R).

2. Appliqué the pieces to the backgrounds. Make 84.

Appliqué feathers. Make 84.

3. Appliqué the reverse pieces to the backgrounds. Make 84.

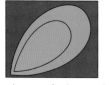

Appliqué reverse feathers. Make 84.

PUTTING IT ALL TOGETHER

1. Arrange and sew together the appliquéd blocks and the rectangles into 12 vertical rows of 14 appliqué blocks and 14 rectangles each. Press.

2. Sew together the rows to form the quilt top. Press.

FINISHING

1. Layer the quilt top with the batting and backing. Baste or pin.

2. Quilt as desired and bind.

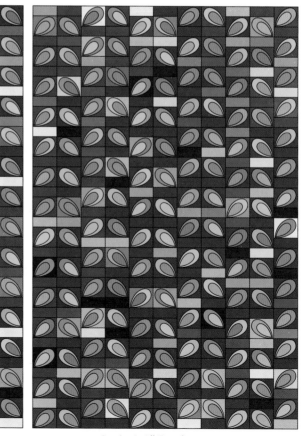

Putting It All Together

JUBILEE LAP QUILT

FINISHED BLOCK: 10″ × 10″ • **FINISHED LAP QUILT:** 60½″ × 80½″

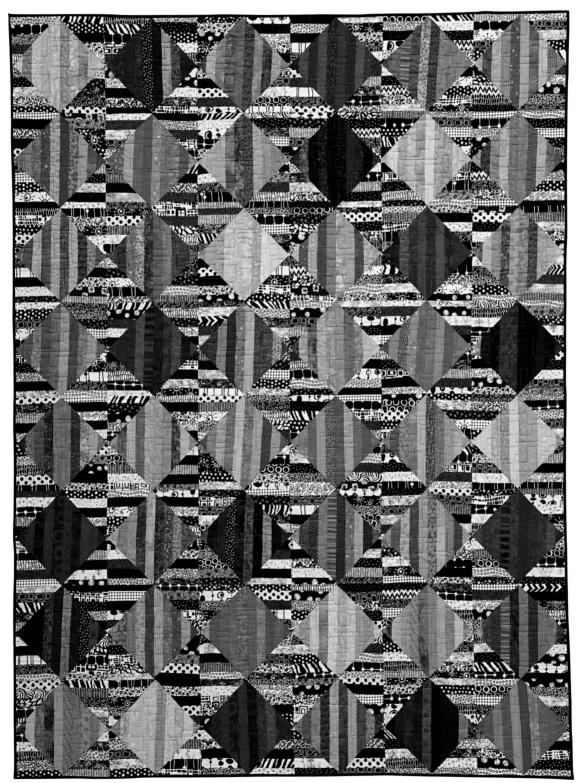

Quilted by Diane Minkley of Patched Works, Inc.

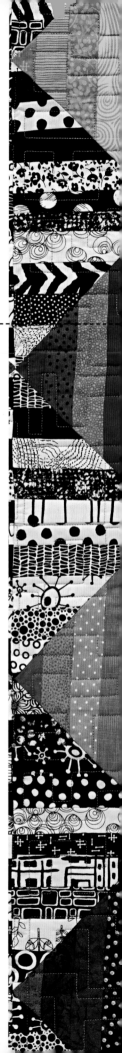

A combination of assorted bright fabrics is used with black-and-white prints in this festive pieced lap quilt. This pattern could also be made using variations of a single color for the pieced centers.

MATERIALS

- ⅝ yard total each of assorted yellows, oranges, reds, pinks, purples, blues, greens, and teals for pieced blocks
- 4½ yards total assorted black-and-white prints for pieced blocks
- 5 yards for backing and binding
- 65″ × 85″ batting

CUTTING

Cut from each assorted color:

- 12 rectangles 1½″ × 11″
- 12 rectangles 1½″ × 9″
- 12 rectangles 1½″ × 7″
- 12 rectangles 1½″ × 5″
- 12 rectangles 1½″ × 3″

Cut from assorted black-and-white prints:

- 576 rectangles 1½″ × 6½″

PIECING

1. Piece the black-and-white rectangles as shown. Make 96 sets of 6 rectangles each. Press.

Piece rectangles. Make 96 sets.

2. Trim the pieced sets to form 96 squares 5⅞″ × 5⅞″.

Trim to make 5⅞″ × 5⅞″ squares.

3. Cut 48 squares diagonally once from lower right to upper left to form 96 triangles.

Cut squares diagonally.

4. Cut 48 squares diagonally once from lower left to upper right to form 96 triangles.

Cut squares diagonally.

5. Center and sew together the assorted colored strips. Press. Make 6 sets per color.

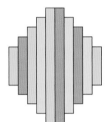

Piece colored sections. Make 6 per color.

6. Trim the pieced sections to create 48 squares 7½″ × 7½″.

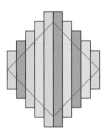

Trim to make 48 squares 7½″ × 7½″.

7. Piece the blocks. Press. Make 6 blocks each per color, for a total of 48 blocks.

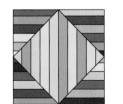

Piece blocks. Make 48 blocks.

PUTTING IT ALL TOGETHER

1. Arrange and sew together the blocks into 8 rows of 6 blocks each. Press.

2. Sew together the rows to form the quilt top. Press.

FINISHING

1. Layer the quilt top with the batting and backing. Baste or pin.

2. Quilt as desired and bind.

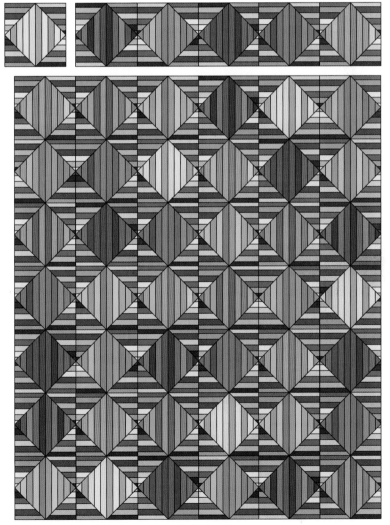

Putting It All Together

TILE WORKS LAP QUILT

FINISHED BLOCK: 9″ × 9″ • **FINISHED LAP QUILT:** 63½″ × 83½″

Quilted by Diane Minkley of Patched Works, Inc.

This quilt is constructed using a single, simple pieced block plus added horizontal and vertical lattice strips. Rotating the block position makes it look more complex than it really is.

MATERIALS

- 3 yards total assorted blacks, black-and-tan prints, and grays for pieced blocks
- 2¾ yards light for pieced blocks, lattice, and border
- 5½ yards for backing and binding
- 68" × 88" batting

CUTTING

Cut from assorted blacks, black-and-tan prints, and grays:

- 48 rectangles 1½" × 5½"
- 48 rectangles 2½" × 5½"
- 48 rectangles 2½" × 4½"
- 48 rectangles 3½" × 4½"
- 48 rectangles 4½" × 6½"

Cut from light:

- 96 rectangles 1½" × 4½" for pieced blocks
- 48 rectangles 1½" × 5½" for pieced blocks
- 48 rectangles 1½" × 9½" for pieced blocks
- 40 rectangles 1½" × 9½" for vertical lattice pieces
- 7 strips 1½" × 59½" for horizontal lattice pieces
- 2 strips 2½" × 79½" for side borders
- 2 strips 2½" × 63½" for top and bottom borders

PIECING

Piece the blocks as shown. Press. Make 48 blocks.

Step 1

Step 2

Step 3

Step 4

Step 5

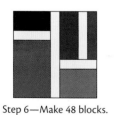

Step 6—Make 48 blocks.

PUTTING IT ALL TOGETHER

QUILT CENTER

1. Arrange the blocks in 8 rows of 6 blocks each.

2. Sew the vertical lattice pieces between the blocks. Press.

3. Sew the horizontal lattice pieces between the rows to form the quilt top. Press.

BORDER

1. Sew the 2 side borders to the quilt top. Press.

2. Sew the top and bottom borders to the quilt top. Press.

FINISHING

1. Layer the quilt top with the batting and backing. Baste or pin.

2. Quilt as desired and bind.

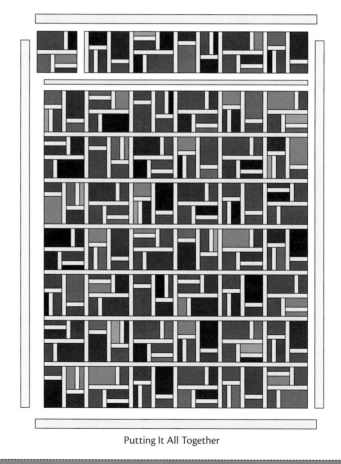

Putting It All Together

TOTALLY STACKED LAP QUILT

FINISHED LAP QUILT: 59½" × 80½"

Quilted by Diane Minkley of Patched Works, Inc.

This vertically oriented lap quilt is super simple to piece, making it a great choice for beginning quilters. The pattern can be constructed as shown, or the rows can be pieced in random order using the listed number of rectangles and squares for each vertical row.

MATERIALS

- 1¾ yards total assorted white-and-black prints (light backgrounds) for pieced rows
- 1½ yards total assorted black-and-white prints (dark backgrounds) for pieced rows
- 1⅞ yards blue for lattice pieces
- 5 yards for backing and binding
- 64" × 85" batting

CUTTING

Cut from assorted white-and-black prints (light backgrounds):
- 20 rectangles 3½" × 5½"
- 28 squares 5½" × 5½"
- 20 rectangles 2½" × 5½"
- 20 rectangles 4½" × 5½"

Cut from blue for lattice pieces:
- 16 strips 3½" × 80½"

Cut from assorted black-and-white prints (dark backgrounds):
- 15 rectangles 2½" × 5½"
- 15 rectangles 4½" × 5½"
- 21 squares 5½" × 5½"
- 15 rectangles 3½" × 5½"

PIECING

1. Arrange and sew the light background rectangles and squares into 4 vertical rows. Use 5 of each of the 3 rectangle sizes and 7 squares per strip. Press.

2. Arrange and sew the dark background rectangles and squares into 3 vertical rows. Use 5 of each of the 3 rectangle sizes and 7 squares per strip. Press.

PUTTING IT ALL TOGETHER

Sew the lattice pieces between the rows and on the sides to form the quilt top. Press.

FINISHING

1. Layer the quilt top with the batting and backing. Baste or pin.

2. Quilt as desired and bind.

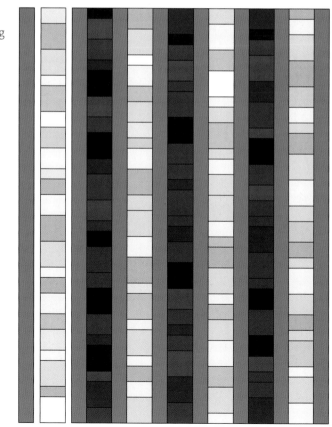

Putting It All Together

STRING OF CIRCLES WALL QUILT

FINISHED BLOCK SIZES: **A:** $6'' \times 10''$ **B:** $6'' \times 10''$ **C:** $9'' \times 10''$ • **FINISHED WALL QUILT:** $42\frac{1}{2}'' \times 40\frac{1}{2}''$

Quilted by Diane Minkley of Patched Works, Inc.

The background for this quilt, which is pieced using assorted black-and-white prints, creates a canvas for the contrasting appliquéd circles. Simple shapes and contrasting fabrics give this wall quilt a more contemporary look.

MATERIALS

- 2½ yards total assorted black-and-white prints for pieced blocks
- ⅛ yard black for appliquéd string
- ⅓ yard total assorted oranges for appliquéd circles
- ¾ yard paper-backed fusible web
- 2⅝ yards for backing and binding
- 47″ × 45″ batting

CUTTING

Cut from assorted black-and-white prints:

- 16 rectangles 3½″ × 5½″ for Block A
- 8 rectangles 5½″ × 6½″ for Block A
- 8 rectangles 2½″ × 7½″ for Block B
- 8 rectangles 3½″ × 4½″ for Block B
- 8 rectangles 3½″ × 6½″ for Block B
- 8 squares 4½″ × 4½″ for Block B
- 16 rectangles 2½″ × 3½″ for Block C
- 8 rectangles 4½″ × 5½″ for Block C
- 8 squares 3½″ × 3½″ for Block C
- 8 rectangles 3½″ × 5½″ for Block C
- 8 rectangles 2½″ × 8½″ for Block C
- 16 rectangles 1½″ × 2½″ for Block C

PIECING

BLOCK A

Piece Block A as shown. Press. Make 8 blocks.

Block A: Step 1

Step 2—Make 8 blocks.

BLOCK B

Piece Block B as shown. Press. Make 8 blocks.

Block B: Step 1

Step 2

Step 3—Make 8 blocks.

BLOCK C

Piece Block C as shown. Press. Make 8 blocks.

Block C: Step 1

Step 2

Step 3

Step 4

Step 5

Step 6

Step 7—Make 8 blocks.

PUTTING IT ALL TOGETHER

1. Arrange and sew together the blocks in 4 rows of 6 blocks each. Use 2 of each block per row. Press.

2. Sew together the rows to form the quilt top. Press.

APPLIQUÉING

Refer to Appliqué (page 5) as needed. Appliqué patterns are on pullout page P2.

1. Cut and prepare:

- 1 each of appliqué pieces 2–6 (3˝ circle, 4˝ circle, 5˝ circle, 6˝ circle, and 7˝ circle)

- 2 of appliqué piece 7 (8˝ circle)

- 1 strip ½˝ × 40½˝ for the string

2. Appliqué the pieces to the quilt top.

FINISHING

1. Layer the quilt top with the batting and backing. Baste or pin.

2. Quilt as desired and bind.

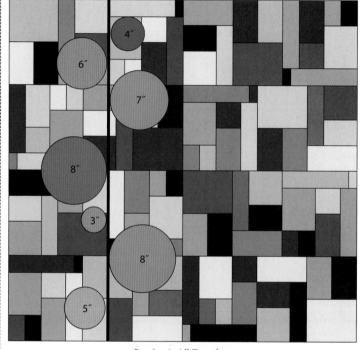

Putting It All Together

INTERWEAVE WALL QUILT

FINISHED BLOCK: $8'' \times 8''$ • **FINISHED WALL QUILT:** $56\frac{1}{2}'' \times 56\frac{1}{2}''$

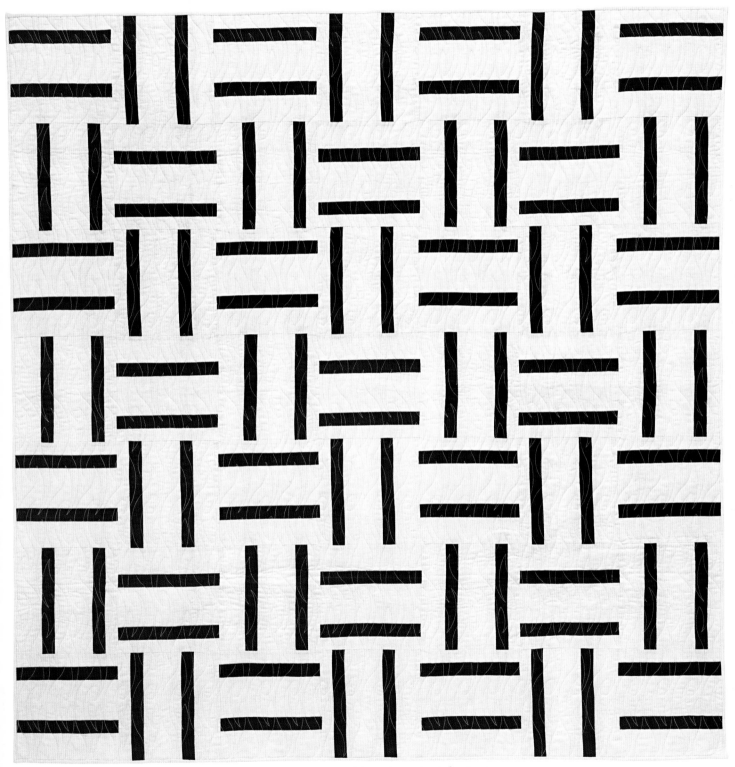

Quilted by Diane Minkley of Patched Works, Inc.

MATERIALS

- 2 yards light for pieced blocks
- 1¼ yards black for pieced blocks
- 3½ yards for backing and binding
- 61″ × 61″ batting

CUTTING

Cut from light:

- 49 rectangles 1½″ × 8½″
- 49 rectangles 3½″ × 8½″
- 49 rectangles 2½″ × 8½″

Cut from black:

- 98 rectangles 1½″ × 8½″

The combination of black and white is a classic for good reason, as quilts made from these fabrics have a timeless appeal. This quilt, which uses only black fabric and creamy white fabric and just one block design, has a very graphic look.

PIECING

Piece the blocks. Press. Make 49 blocks.

Piece blocks. Make 49 blocks.

PUTTING IT ALL TOGETHER

1. Arrange and sew together the blocks in 7 rows of 7 blocks each. Press.

2. Sew together the rows to form the quilt top. Press.

FINISHING

1. Layer the quilt top with the batting and backing. Baste or pin.

2. Quilt as desired and bind.

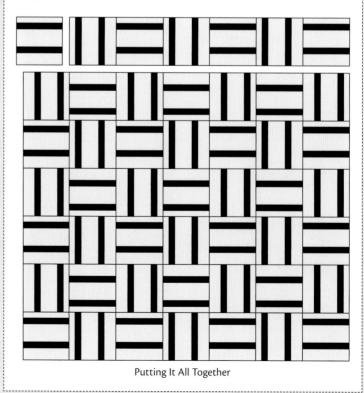

Putting It All Together

PAINTBOX CIRCLES WALL QUILT

FINISHED BLOCK: $8'' \times 8''$ • **FINISHED WALL QUILT:** $40\frac{1}{2}'' \times 40\frac{1}{2}''$

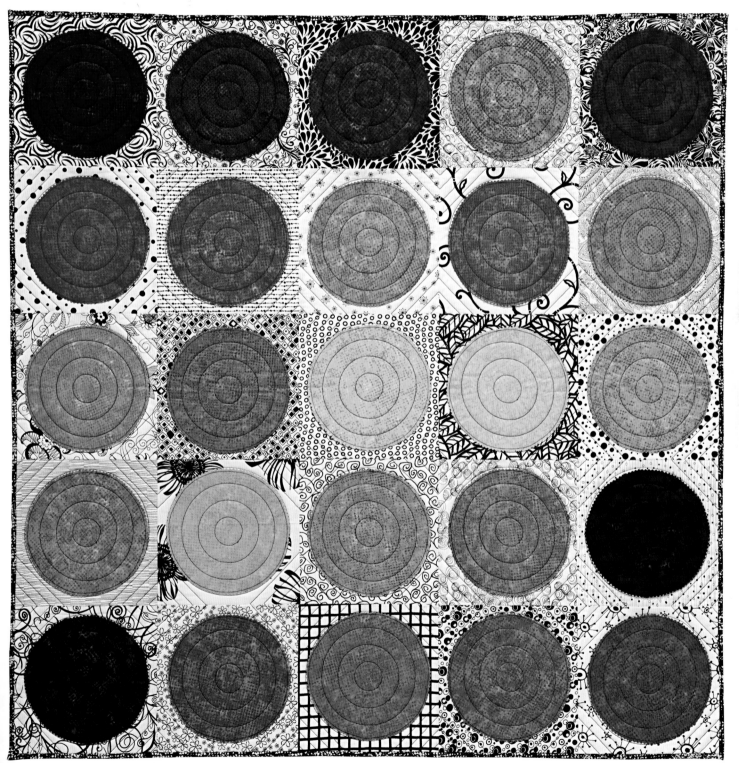

Quilted by Diane Minkley of Patched Works, Inc.

MATERIALS

- 2 yards total assorted black-and-white prints for appliqué backgrounds

- 1⅓ yards total assorted brights for appliquéd circles

- 2⅝ yards for backing and binding

- 3 yards paper-backed fusible web

- 45″ × 45″ batting

CUTTING

Cut from assorted black-and-white prints:

- 25 squares 8½″ × 8½″

This fun quilt is fast and easy

to complete. Raw-edge appliqué is a great alternative for all of you appliqué-apprehensive quilters! Here the circles can be cut using pinking shears, and then raw-edge appliquéd. What could be easier?

APPLIQUÉING

Refer to Appliqué (page 5) as needed. Appliqué patterns are on pullout page P2.

1. Cut and prepare 25 of appliqué piece 6 (7″ circle). For raw-edge appliqué, cut using pinking shears.

2. Appliqué the pieces to the backgrounds. For raw-edge appliqué, use a straight stitch to sew ⅛″ from the outer edge of the circles.

Appliqué circles. Make 25 blocks.

PUTTING IT ALL TOGETHER

1. Arrange and sew together the blocks in 5 rows of 5 blocks each. Press.

2. Sew together the rows to form the quilt top. Press.

FINISHING

1. Layer the quilt top with the batting and backing. Baste or pin.

2. Quilt as desired and bind.

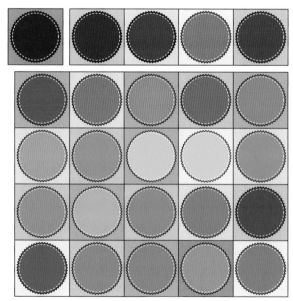

Putting It All Together

THIS AND THAT WALL QUILT

FINISHED BLOCK: 10″ × 10″ • **FINISHED WALL QUILT:** 50½″ × 50½″

Quilted by Diane Minkley of Patched Works, Inc.

Two alternating pieced blocks make up this simple-to-cut and easy-to-piece wall quilt. Contrast within the blocks is the key to success with this pattern.

MATERIALS

- 1½ yards total assorted white-and-black prints (light backgrounds) for pieced blocks

- 1 yard total assorted black-and-white prints (dark backgrounds) for pieced blocks

- ⅞ yard total assorted pinks for pieced blocks

- 3⅛ yards for backing and binding

- 55" × 55" batting

CUTTING

Cut from assorted white-and-black prints (light backgrounds):

- 26 rectangles 3½" × 6½" for Block A

- 24 rectangles 1½" × 8½" for Block A

- 24 rectangles 1½" × 10½" for Block B

Cut from assorted black-and-white prints (dark backgrounds):

- 26 rectangles 2½" × 6½" for Block A

- 52 rectangles 2½" × 5½" for Block A

Cut from assorted pinks:

- 12 squares 8½" × 8½" for Block B

PIECING

BLOCK A

Piece Block A as shown.
Press. Make 13 blocks.

Block A: Step 1

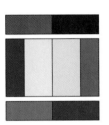

Step 2

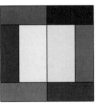

Step 3—Make 13 blocks.

BLOCK B

Piece Block B as shown.
Press. Make 12 blocks.

Block B: Step 1.

Step 2—Make 12 blocks.

PUTTING IT ALL TOGETHER

1. Arrange and sew together the blocks in 5 rows of 5 blocks each. Press.

2. Sew together the rows to form the quilt top. Press.

FINISHING

1. Layer the quilt top with the batting and backing. Baste or pin.

2. Quilt as desired and bind.

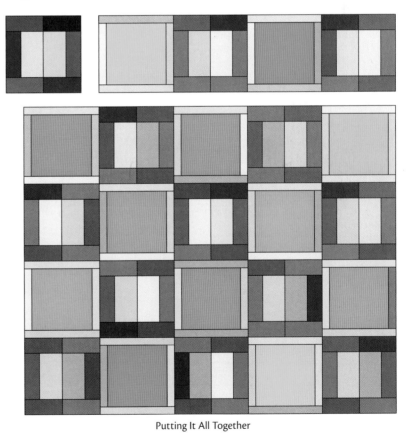

Putting It All Together

MIDNIGHT MOON WALL QUILT

FINISHED BLOCK: 10″ × 10″ • **FINISHED WALL QUILT:** 40½″ × 40½″

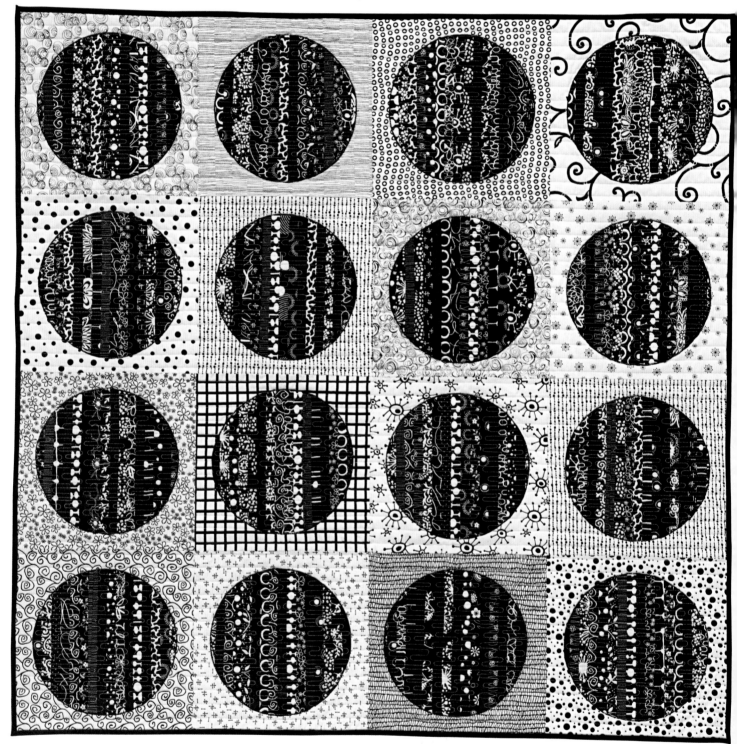

Quilted by Diane Minkley of Patched Works, Inc.

Strip-pieced appliquéd circles are the focus of this classic wall quilt made using just black-and-white prints.

MATERIALS

- 2 yards total assorted white-and-black prints (light backgrounds) for appliqué block backgrounds
- 2 yards total assorted black-and-white prints (dark backgrounds) for appliquéd circles
- 2⅝ yards for backing and binding
- 2 yards paper-backed fusible web
- 45″ × 45″ batting

CUTTING

Cut from assorted white-and-black prints (light backgrounds):
- 16 squares 10½″ × 10½″

Cut from assorted black-and-white prints (dark backgrounds):
- 256 strips 1″ × 9″

PIECING

Arrange and sew together 16 sets of 16 strips each for the appliquéd circles. Press.

Piece rectangles. Make 16 sets.

APPLIQUÉING

Refer to Appliqué (page 5) as needed. Appliqué patterns are on pullout page P2.

1. Cut and prepare 16 of appliqué piece 7 (8″ circle) using the pieced strips.

2. Center and appliqué the pieces to the backgrounds.

Appliqué circles. Make 16 blocks.

PUTTING IT ALL TOGETHER

1. Arrange and sew together the blocks in 4 rows of 4 blocks each. Press.

2. Sew together the rows to form the quilt top. Press.

FINISHING

1. Layer the quilt top with the batting and backing. Baste or pin.

2. Quilt as desired and bind.

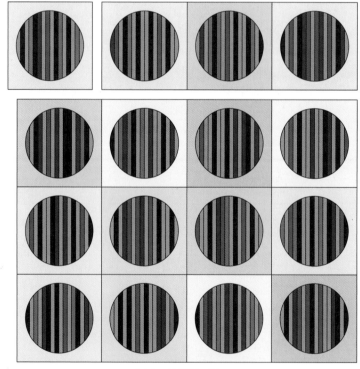

Putting It All Together

CHECKERED PAST RUNNER

FINISHED RUNNER: 16½" × 46½"

DETAIL

Quilted by Diane Minkley of Patched Works, Inc.

MATERIALS

- 1 yard total assorted black-and-white prints
- ⅓ yard total assorted brights
- 1½ yards for backing and binding
- 21″ × 51″ batting

CUTTING

Cut from assorted black-and-white prints:

- 165 squares 2½″ × 2½″

Cut from assorted brights:

- 19 squares 2½″ × 2½″

Bright fabrics are combined with black-and-white prints in this simple yet stylish runner made using all 2½″ squares.

PUTTING IT ALL TOGETHER

1. Arrange and sew together 23 rows of 8 squares each. Press.

2. Arrange and sew together the pieced rows to form the runner top. Press.

FINISHING

1. Layer the runner top with the batting and backing. Baste or pin.

2. Quilt as desired and bind.

Putting It All Together

PAIRED SQUARES RUNNER

FINISHED BLOCK: 12″ × 12″ • **FINISHED RUNNER:** 18½″ × 83½″

DETAIL

Quilted by Diane Minkley of Patched Works, Inc.

Black-and-white fabrics are paired with browns and tans to create this classically elegant runner.

MATERIALS

- ¼ yard total assorted tans for pieced blocks
- Scraps of assorted browns for pieced blocks
- 1 yard light for pieced blocks, lattice, and border
- ¾ yard total assorted black-and-white prints for pieced blocks
- 2½ yards for backing and binding
- 23″ × 88″ batting

CUTTING

Cut from assorted tans:
- 4 squares 6½″ × 6½″ for Block A

Cut from assorted browns:
- 2 squares 4½″ × 4½″ for Block B

Cut from light:
- 12 rectangles 1½″ × 6½″ for Blocks A and B
- 8 rectangles 1½″ × 8½″ for Block A
- 4 rectangles 1½″ × 4½″ for Block B
- 5 rectangles 1½″ × 12½″ for lattice
- 2 strips 3½″ × 77½″ for side borders
- 2 strips 3½″ × 18½″ for end borders

Cut from assorted black-and-white prints:
- 8 rectangles 2½″ × 8½″ for Block A
- 8 rectangles 2½″ × 12½″ for Block A
- 4 rectangles 3½″ × 6½″ for Block B
- 4 rectangles 3½″ × 12½″ for Block B

PIECING

BLOCK A
Piece Block A as shown. Make 4 blocks.

Block A: Step 1

Step 2

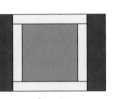
Step 3

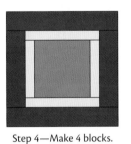
Step 4—Make 4 blocks.

BLOCK B
Piece Block B as shown. Make 2 blocks.

Block B: Step 1

Step 2

Step 3

Step 4—Make 2 blocks.

FINISHING

1. Layer the runner top with the batting and backing. Baste or pin.

2. Quilt as desired and bind.

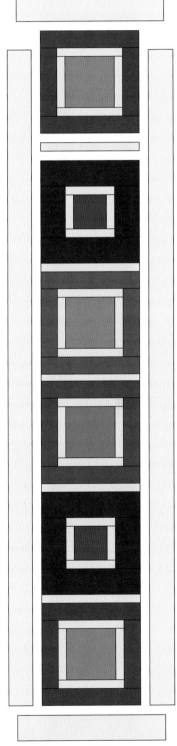
Putting It All Together

PUTTING IT ALL TOGETHER

1. Arrange the blocks in 1 row.

2. Sew the lattice pieces between the blocks to form the runner top. Press.

3. Sew the 2 side borders to the runner top. Press.

4. Sew the end borders to the runner top. Press.

MARTINI RUNNER

FINISHED RUNNER: 20½″ × 60½″

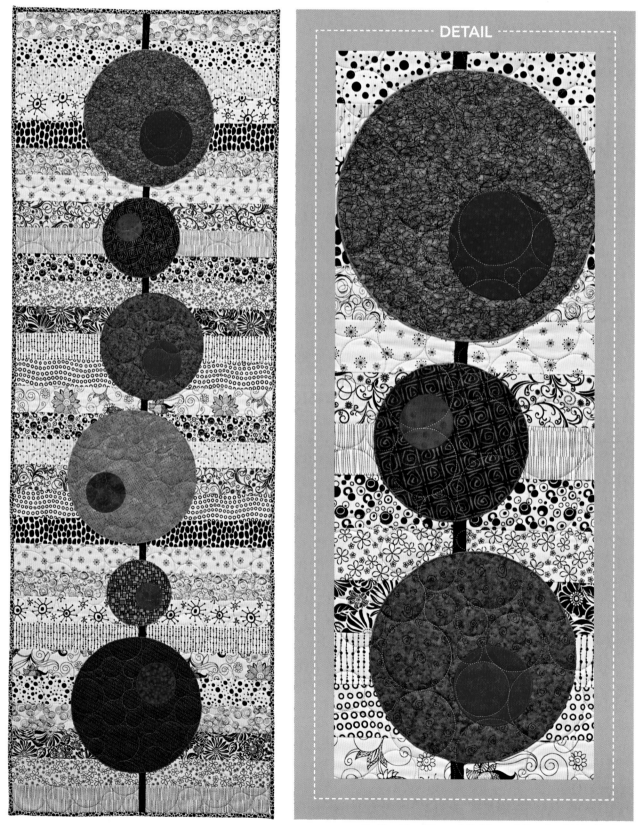

DETAIL

Black & White, Bright & Bold

Quilted by Diane Minkley of Patched Works, Inc.

Black-and-white prints make up the pieced background for this whimsical appliquéd runner. Use green and red fabrics for the circles to make them look like olives!

MATERIALS

- 1⅓ yards total assorted black-and-white prints for pieced background
- ½ yard total assorted greens for appliquéd circles
- ⅛ yard total assorted reds for appliquéd circles
- ⅛ yard black for appliquéd string
- 1⅞ yards for backing and binding
- 1½ yards paper-backed fusible web
- 25″ × 65″ batting

CUTTING

Cut from assorted black-and-white prints:

- 30 rectangles 2½″ × 20½″

PUTTING IT ALL TOGETHER

Arrange and sew together the rectangles in 1 row of 30 rectangles to form the runner top. Press.

APPLIQUÉING

Refer to Appliqué (page 5) as needed. Appliqué patterns are on pullout page P2.

1. Cut and prepare:

- 2 of appliqué piece 1 (2″ circle)
- 3 of appliqué piece 2 (3″ circle)
- 1 each of appliqué pieces 3–5 (4″ circle, 5″ circle, 6″ circle)
- 1 of appliqué piece 7 (8″ circle)
- 3 of appliqué piece 8 (10″ circle)
- 2 of appliqué piece 9
- 5 of appliqué piece 10

2. Appliqué the appropriate pieces to the runner top.

FINISHING

1. Layer the runner top with the batting and backing. Baste or pin.

2. Quilt as desired and bind.

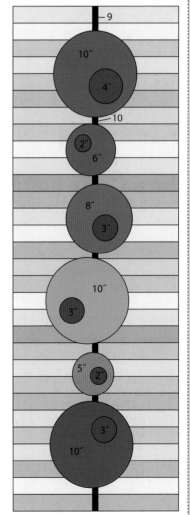

Putting It All Together

BOARDWALK RUNNER

FINISHED RUNNER: 20½" × 53½"

DETAIL

Black & White, Bright & Bold

Quilted by Diane Minkley of Patched Works, Inc.

Purples and teals are combined with black-and-white prints in this easy-to-piece runner.

MATERIALS

- ½ yard total assorted purples for pieced sections
- ⅓ yard total assorted teals for pieced sections
- ¾ yard total assorted black-and-white prints
- 1⅔ yards for backing and binding
- 25″ × 58″ batting

CUTTING

Cut from assorted purples:
- 40 rectangles 2½″ × 3½″

Cut from assorted teals:
- 30 rectangles 2½″ × 3½″

Cut from assorted black-and-white prints:
- 8 rectangles 4½″ × 20½″

PIECING

1. Arrange and sew together 4 rows of 10 rectangles each from the assorted purples. Press.

2. Arrange and sew together 3 rows of 10 rectangles each from the assorted teals. Press.

PUTTING IT ALL TOGETHER

Arrange and sew together the pieced sections between the black-and-white rectangles to form the runner top. Press.

FINISHING

1. Layer the runner top with the batting and backing. Baste or pin.

2. Quilt as desired and bind.

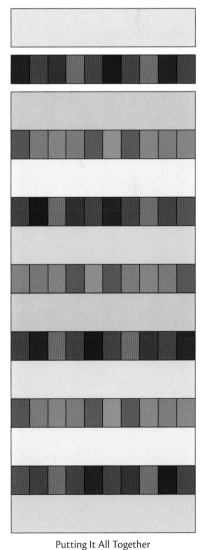

Putting It All Together

BERRY VINE RUNNER

FINISHED RUNNER: 24½″ × 58½″

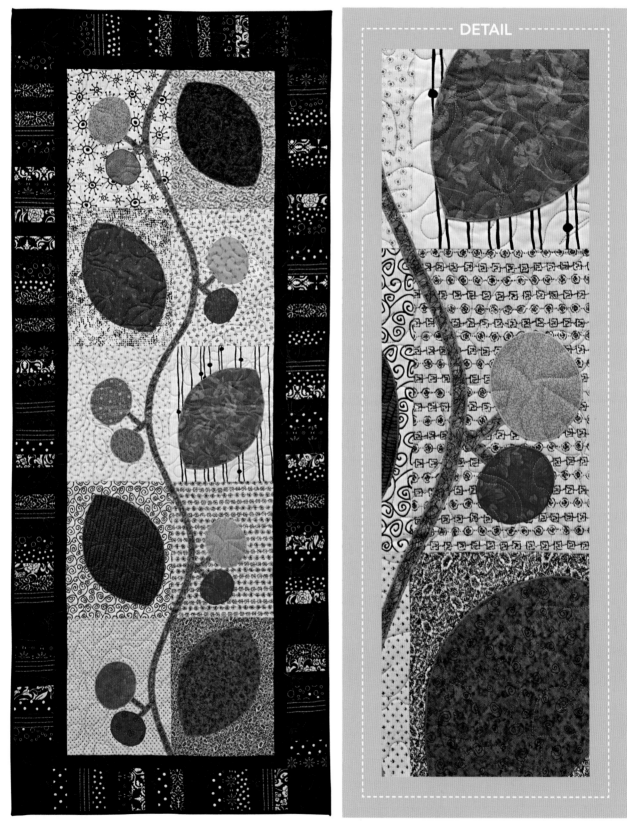

DETAIL

Black & White, Bright & Bold

Quilted by Diane Minkley of Patched Works, Inc.

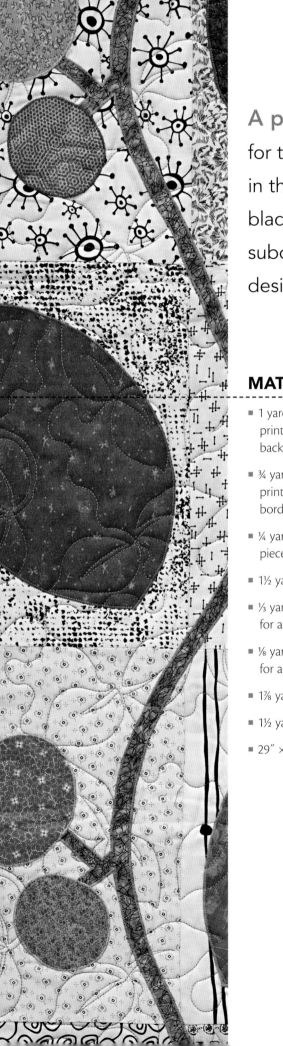

A pieced border provides a frame

for the appliquéd oversize leaves and berries in this traditional runner. The combination of black-and-cream fabrics gives it a softer, more subdued look. I turned one leaf to make the design less directional.

MATERIALS

- 1 yard total assorted white-and-black prints (light backgrounds) for pieced background
- ¾ yard total assorted black-and-white prints (dark backgrounds) for pieced border
- ¼ yard black for inner border and pieced border corner squares
- 1½ yards green for appliquéd vine
- ⅓ yard total assorted greens for appliquéd leaves
- ⅛ yard total assorted pinks for appliquéd berries
- 1⅞ yards for backing and binding
- 1½ yards paper-backed fusible web
- 29″ × 63″ batting

CUTTING

Cut from assorted white-and-black prints (light backgrounds):

- 10 rectangles 8½″ × 10½″

Cut from assorted black-and-white prints (dark backgrounds):

- 140 rectangles 1½″ × 3½″

Cut from black:

- 2 strips 1½″ × 50½″ for side inner borders
- 2 strips 1½″ × 18½″ for end inner borders
- 4 squares 3½″ × 3½″ for pieced border corner squares

PIECING

1. Arrange and sew 5 rows of 2 blocks each for the background. Press.

2. Sew the rows together to form the background. Press.

3. Arrange and sew together 2 rows of 52 rectangles each for the 2 side pieced borders. Press.

4. Arrange and sew together 2 rows of 18 rectangles each for the 2 end pieced borders. Press.

5. Sew a corner square to each end of the end border pieces to form the runner top. Press.

APPLIQUÉING

Refer to Appliqué (page 5) as needed. Appliqué patterns are on pullout page P1.

1. Cut and prepare:

- 1 of appliqué piece 1 (connect the ends of the partial pattern for the full vine)

- 5 each of appliqué pieces 2–4

2. Appliqué the pieces to the background.

PUTTING IT ALL TOGETHER

1. Sew the 2 side inner borders to the runner top. Press.

2. Sew the 2 end inner borders to the runner top. Press.

3. Sew the 2 side pieced borders to the runner top. Press.

4. Sew the 2 end pieced borders to the runner top. Press.

FINISHING

1. Layer the runner top with the batting and backing. Baste or pin.

2. Quilt as desired and bind.

Putting It All Together

CROOKED PATH RUNNER

FINISHED RUNNER: 20½″ × 50½″

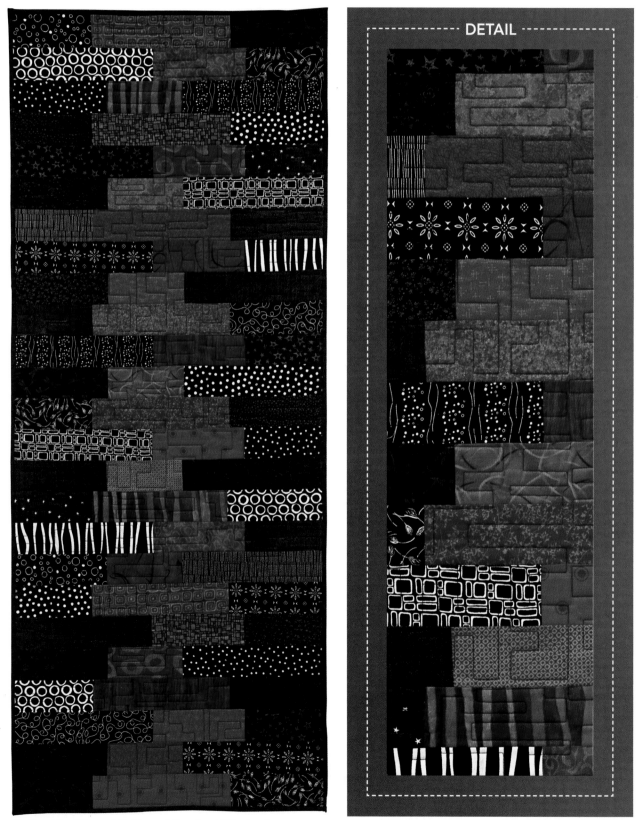

DETAIL

Quilted by Diane Minkley of Patched Works, Inc.

MATERIALS

- 1 yard total assorted black-and-white prints
- ¾ yard total assorted reds
- 1⅝ yards for backing and binding
- 25" × 55" batting

CUTTING

Cut from assorted black-and-white prints:

- 17 rectangles 2½" × 5½"
- 17 rectangles 2½" × 6½"
- 16 rectangles 2½" × 9½"

Cut from assorted reds:

- 8 rectangles 2½" × 5½"
- 8 rectangles 2½" × 6½"
- 9 rectangles 2½" × 9½"

This runner is fast and fun to make. The combination of reds with black and white creates a timeless classic.

PIECING

1. Arrange and sew together the rectangles in 3 rows of 3 rectangles each as shown. Press. Make 8 sections.

Make 8 sections.

2. Make a single row of 3 rectangles in the same arrangement as the top row of the sections.

PUTTING IT ALL TOGETHER

Sew together the sections, adding the single row at the bottom, to form the runner top. Press.

FINISHING

1. Layer the runner top with the batting and backing. Baste or pin.

2. Quilt as desired and bind.

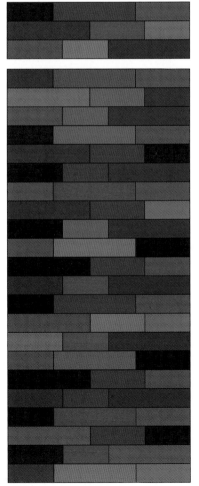

Putting It All Together

LIGHTS OUT RUNNER

FINISHED RUNNER: 21½″ × 63½″

DETAIL

Quilted by Diane Minkley of Patched Works, Inc.

The classic combination of black and white is used in this pieced runner with timeless appeal.

MATERIALS

- 1 yard black for blocks and end borders
- 1 yard light for lattice and borders
- 2 yards for backing and binding
- 26″ × 68″ batting

CUTTING

Cut from black:

- 70 squares 3½″ × 3½″ for blocks
- 4 strips 1½″ × 21½″ for end borders

Cut from light:

- 60 rectangles 1½″ × 3½″ for vertical lattice
- 13 rectangles 1½″ × 19½″ for horizontal lattice
- 2 strips 1½″ × 49½″ for side borders
- 4 strips 1½″ × 21½″ for end borders

1. Arrange the blocks in 12 rows of 5 blocks each.

2. Sew the vertical lattice pieces between the blocks and on the ends. Press.

Sew lattice pieces between blocks.

3. Sew the horizontal lattice pieces between the rows and on the ends. Press.

4. Sew the 2 side borders to the runner top. Press.

5. Arrange the remaining blocks in 2 rows of 5 blocks each for the end borders.

6. Sew the vertical lattice pieces between and on each end of the border blocks. Press.

7. Sew the horizontal lattice pieces and border pieces to the border rows to form the runner top. Press.

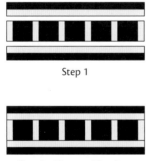

Step 1

Step 2—Piece end borders.

8. Sew the end borders to the runner top. Press.

1. Layer the runner top with the batting and backing. Baste or pin.

2. Quilt as desired and bind.

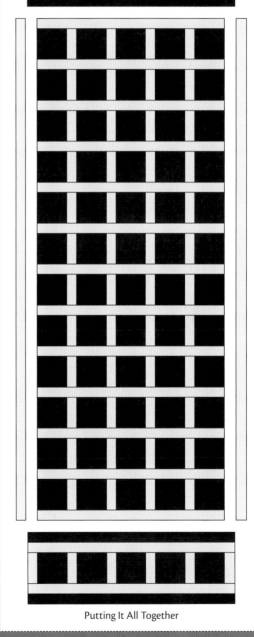

Putting It All Together

PLACE MATS

Mix and match a set of place mats for yourself or to give as a gift to someone special. There are six different designs to choose from.

SIDEBAR PLACE MAT

FINISHED PLACE MAT: 16½″ × 12½″

Quilted by Diane Minkley of Patched Works, Inc.

PUTTING IT ALL TOGETHER

1. Arrange and sew together the vertical rows. Press.

2. Sew together the rows. Press.

3. Sew the inner borders to the center. Press.

4. Arrange and sew together 2 rows of 6 rectangles each for the 2 pieced borders to form the place mat. Press.

5. Sew the pieced borders to the place mat. Press.

FINISHING

1. Layer the place mat with the batting and backing. Baste or pin.

2. Quilt as desired and bind.

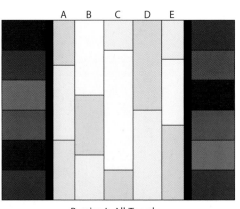

Putting It All Together

MATERIALS

- ¼ yard total assorted white-and-black prints (light backgrounds) for pieced center

- ⅛ yard total assorted black-and-white prints (dark backgrounds) for pieced borders

- ⅛ yard black for inner border

- ¾ yard for backing and binding

- 20″ × 16″ batting

CUTTING

Cut from assorted white-and-black prints (light backgrounds):

- 2 rectangles 2″ × 3½″ (1 each for Rows A and E)

- 2 rectangles 2″ × 4½″ (1 each for Rows A and E)

- 2 rectangles 2″ × 5½″ (1 each for Rows A and E)

- 1 rectangle 2½″ × 3½″ (for Row B)

- 1 rectangle 2½″ × 4½″ (for Row B)

- 1 rectangle 2½″ × 5½″ (for Row B)

- 2 squares 2½″ × 2½″ (for Row C)

- 1 rectangle 2½″ × 8½″ (for Row C)

- 2 rectangles 2½″ × 6½″ (for Row D)

Cut from assorted black-and-white prints (dark backgrounds):

- 12 rectangles 2½″ × 3½″

Cut from black:

- 2 strips 1″ × 12½″

SPOTS PLACE MAT

FINISHED PLACE MAT: $16\frac{1}{2}" \times 12\frac{1}{2}"$

MATERIALS

- ⅓ yard total assorted black-and-white prints for pieced background
- ⅛ yard total assorted brights for appliquéd circles
- ¾ yard for backing and binding
- ⅓ yard paper-backed fusible web
- $20" \times 16"$ batting

CUTTING

Cut from assorted black-and-white prints:

- 12 squares $4\frac{1}{2}" \times 4\frac{1}{2}"$

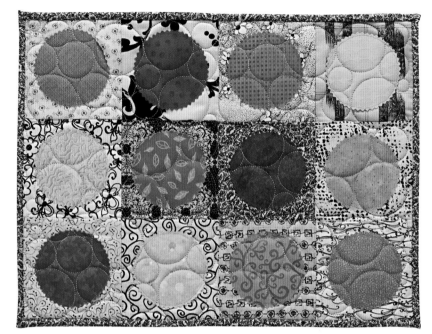

Quilted by Diane Minkley of Patched Works, Inc.

PUTTING IT ALL TOGETHER

Refer to Appliqué (page 5) as needed. Appliqué patterns are on pullout page P2.

PIECING

1. Arrange and sew together 3 rows of 4 squares each. Press.

2. Sew together the rows to form the place mat. Press.

APPLIQUÉING

1. Cut and prepare 12 of appliqué piece 2 (3" circle). For raw-edge appliqué, cut with pinking shears.

2. Appliqué the pieces to the backgrounds. For raw-edge appliqué, use a straight stitch to sew ⅛" from the outer edge of the circles.

FINISHING

1. Layer the place mat with the batting and backing. Baste or pin.

2. Quilt as desired and bind.

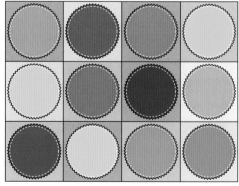

Putting It All Together

CENTER SQUARE PLACE MAT

FINISHED PLACE MAT: 16½″ × 12½″

Quilted by Diane Minkley of Patched Works, Inc.

PUTTING IT ALL TOGETHER

Piece the place mat. Press.

FINISHING

1. Layer the place mat with the batting and backing. Baste or pin.

2. Quilt as desired and bind.

Putting It All Together

MATERIALS

- ¼ yard total assorted white-and-black prints (light backgrounds)
- ¼ yard total assorted black-and-white prints (dark backgrounds)
- ¾ yard for backing and binding
- 20″ × 16″ batting

CUTTING

Cut from assorted white-and-black prints (light backgrounds):

- 4 squares 2½″ × 2½″
- 4 rectangles 2½″ × 4½″
- 4 rectangles 2½″ × 6½″

Cut from assorted black-and-white prints (dark backgrounds):

- 4 squares 2½″ × 2½″
- 4 rectangles 2½″ × 4½″
- 4 rectangles 2½″ × 6½″

FINE VINE PLACE MAT

FINISHED PLACE MAT: 16½" × 12½"

MATERIALS

- ¼ yard black-and-white print (dark background) for appliqué background

- ⅛ yard total assorted greens and teals for appliqué leaves

- ⅜ yard white-and-black print (light background) for center

- ¾ yard for backing and binding

- ⅛ yard paper-backed fusible web

- 20" × 16" batting

CUTTING

Cut from black-and-white print (dark background):

- 1 rectangle 4½" × 12½"

Cut from white-and-black print (light background):

- 1 square 12½" × 12½"

Quilted by Diane Minkley of Patched Works, Inc.

PUTTING IT ALL TOGETHER

Refer to Appliqué (page 5) as needed. Appliqué patterns are on pullout page P2.

APPLIQUÉING

1. Cut and prepare 8 each of appliqué pieces 1 and 2.

2. Appliqué the pieces to the background.

PIECING

Sew the appliqué background to the center to form the place mat. Press.

FINISHING

1. Layer the place mat with the batting and backing. Baste or pin.

2. Quilt as desired and bind.

Putting It All Together

STRIPPY PLACE MAT

FINISHED PLACE MAT: 16½" × 12½"

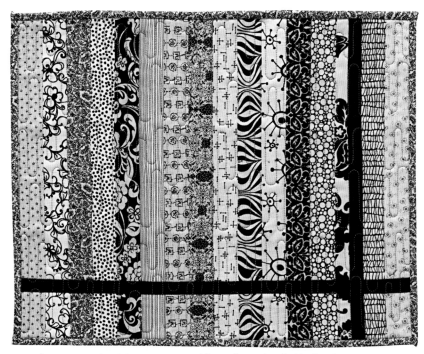

Quilted by Diane Minkley of Patched Works, Inc.

MATERIALS

- ⅓ yard total assorted black-and-white prints for pieced background
- ⅛ yard black for appliqué
- ¾ yard for backing and binding
- ⅛ yard paper-backed fusible web
- 20" × 16" batting

CUTTING

Cut from assorted black-and-white prints:

- 16 strips 1½" × 12½"

PUTTING IT ALL TOGETHER

Refer to Appliqué (page 5) as needed. Appliqué patterns are on pullout page P2.

PIECING

Arrange and sew together the strips to form the background. Press.

APPLIQUÉING

1. Cut and prepare 1 each of appliqué pieces 1 and 2.

2. Appliqué the pieces to the background to form the place mat.

FINISHING

1. Layer the place mat with the batting and backing. Baste or pin.

2. Quilt as desired and bind.

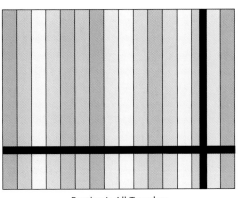

Putting It All Together

COLOR BAR PLACE MAT

FINISHED PLACE MAT: 16½" × 12½"

MATERIALS

- ¼ yard white-and-black print (light background) for pieced background
- ⅛ yard black print for pieced background
- ⅛ yard total assorted brights for appliqué
- ¾ yard for backing and binding
- ¼ yard paper-backed fusible web
- 20" × 16" batting

CUTTING

Cut from white-and-black print (light background):

- 1 rectangle 8½" × 16½"

Cut from black print:

- 2 rectangles 2½" × 16½"

Quilted by Diane Minkley of Patched Works, Inc.

PUTTING IT ALL TOGETHER

Refer to Appliqué (page 5) as needed. Appliqué patterns are on pullout page P2.

PIECING

Piece the background as shown. Press.

APPLIQUÉING

1. Cut and prepare 64 of appliqué piece 1.

2. Appliqué the pieces to the background to form the place mat.

FINISHING

1. Layer the place mat with the batting and backing. Baste or pin.

2. Quilt as desired and bind.

Piece background.

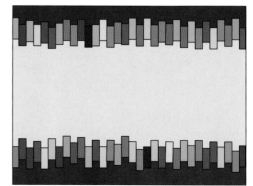

Putting It All Together

ABOUT THE AUTHOR

Kim Schaefer began sewing at an early age and was quilting seriously by the late 1980s. Her early quilting career included designing and producing small quilts for craft shows and shops across the country.

In 1986, Kim founded Little Quilt Company, a pattern company focused on designing a variety of small, fun-to-make projects.

In addition to designing quilt patterns, Kim is a best-selling author for C&T Publishing. Kim also designs fabric for Andover/Makower and works with Leo Licensing, which licenses her designs for nonfabric products.

Kim lives with her family in southeastern Wisconsin.

For more information on Little Quilt Company, please visit www.littlequiltcompany.com, which offers Kim's entire collection of patterns, books, and fabrics.

Little Quilt Company's Facebook page has posts about new patterns, books, and fabrics, and an occasional peek at Kim's latest work.

ALSO BY KIM SCHAEFER:

Available as an eBook only   Available as an eBook only

Great Titles *from* C&T PUBLISHING

Available at your local retailer or **www.ctpub.com** *or* **800-284-1114**

For a list of other fine books from C&T Publishing, visit our website to view our catalog online.

C&T PUBLISHING, INC.
P.O. Box 1456
Lafayette, CA 94549
800-284-1114

Email: ctinfo@ctpub.com
Website: www.ctpub.com

C&T Publishing's professional photography services are now available to the public. Visit us at www.ctmediaservices.com.

Tips and Techniques can be found at www.ctpub.com > Consumer Resources > Quiltmaking Basics: Tips & Techniques for Quiltmaking & More

For quilting supplies:

COTTON PATCH
1025 Brown Ave.
Lafayette, CA 94549
Store: 925-284-1177
Mail order: 925-283-7883

Email: CottonPa@aol.com
Website: www.quiltusa.com

Note: Fabrics shown may not be currently available, as fabric manufacturers keep most fabrics in print for only a short time.